The Journey
Coloring book

Adrienne Trafford

4880 Lower Valley Road · Atglen, Pennsylvania 19310

Schiffer Books are available at special discounts for bulk purchases for sales promotions or premiums. Special editions, including personalized covers, corporate imprints, and excerpts can be created in large quantities for special needs. For more information contact the publisher:

Published by Schiffer Publishing Ltd.
4880 Lower Valley Road
Atglen, PA 19310
Phone: (610) 593-1777; Fax: (610) 593-2002
E-mail: Info@schifferbooks.com

For the largest selection of fine reference books on this and related subjects, please visit our web site at
www.schifferbooks.com
We are always looking for people to write books on new and related subjects. If you have an idea for a book please contact us at the above address.

This book may be purchased from the publisher.
Include $5.00 for shipping.
Please try your bookstore first.
You may write for a free catalog.

In Europe, Schiffer books are distributed by
Bushwood Books
6 Marksbury Ave.
Kew Gardens
Surrey TW9 4JF England
Phone: 44 (0) 20 8392-8585; Fax: 44 (0) 20 8392-9876
E-mail: info@bushwoodbooks.co.uk
Website: www.bushwoodbooks.co.uk

Illustrations by Adrienne Trafford

ISBN: 978-0-7643-3784-0
Printed in China

Appreciation

Beauty

Changes

Confined

Defiance

Desire

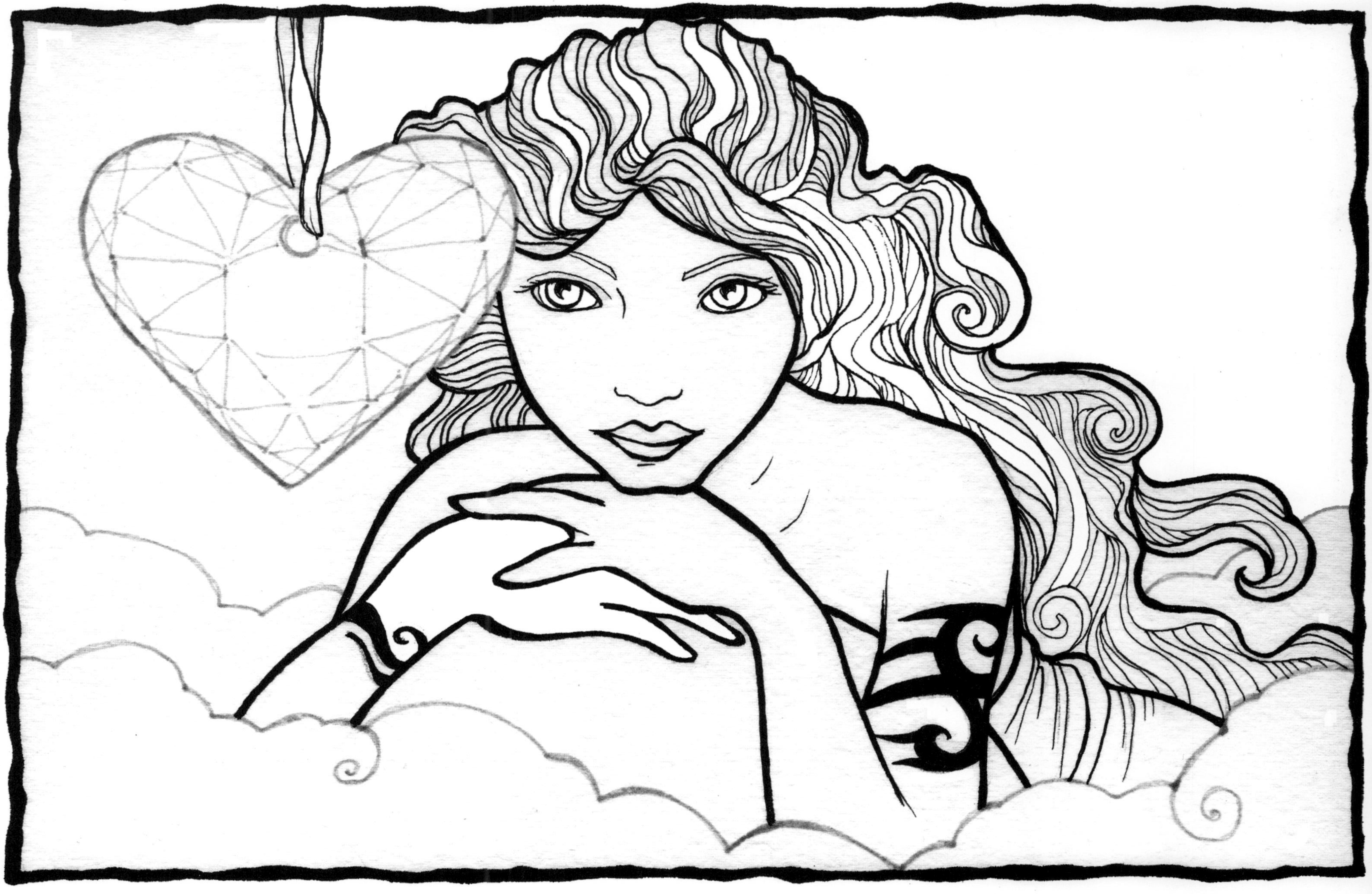

Drifting

Entangled

Eve

Fertility

Fleeting

Home

Hope

Independence

amt.

Innocence

Instinct

Loss

Luxury

Mother Earth

Passion

amt

Patience

Queen of Clubs

Queen of Diamonds

Queen of Hearts

amt

Queen of Spades

Rebirth

Resilience

Storms

Talisman

The Actress

The Adventurer

The Ancestors

The Champion

The Fragile Thread

The Goddess

The Guardian

The Mermaid

The Messenger

amt

The Puppet

The Quiet One

The Radiant One

The Vampire

The Wish

Torn

Welcome